SELF CATERING

(A Short History of the World)

SELF CATERING

(A Short History of the World)

by Andrew Cullen

WARNER CHAPPELL PLAYS

LONDON

A Time Warner Company

Self Catering (A Short History of the World)
First published in 1993
by Warner Chappell Plays Ltd
129 Park Street, London W1Y 3FA

ISBN 0 85676 170 2

Printed by Commercial Colour Press, London E7

SELF CATERING (A Short History of the World) was commissioned in 1990 by Altered States Theatre Company with Arts Council support. The play was first performed at the Liverpool Playhouse Studio on 29th September, 1992, with the following cast:

BETTE DAVIS	Ayse Owens
CLINT EASTWOOD	Andrew Schofield
HENRY FONDA	Paul Broughton
MARILYN MONROE	Rosie Rowell
MERYL STREEP	Jane Hogarth

The production transferred to the Cockpit Theatre, London, opening on 18th January, 1993, with the following cast:

BETTE DAVIS	Ayse Owens
CLINT EASTWOOD	Mark Spalding
HENRY FONDA	John Griffin
MARILYN MONROE	Matilda Zeigler
MERYL STREEP	Jane Hogarth

Directed by Kate Rowland

Designed by Hannah Mayall

Music by Martin Dempsey

Lighting by Johanna Town

When one character starts speaking before the other has finished, the point of interruption is marked /

Scene One

*Blackness. The sound of violent wind and rain. The sound of
an aeroplane hurtling towards the ground and crashing in the
midst of the storm.*

Scene Two

*The empty beach. A tumult of voices off stage. The first four
speeches are spoken simultaneously.*

MARILYN   Oh God, oh God, oh God. What happened?
Where are we? Does anyone know where we are?
What does my hair look like? Is it a complete
mess? Oh God, I just want to sit down and I
don't want anyone to look at my hair until I've
had five minutes with it. That's all you need with
my hair. I'm lucky that way. You might not think
so to look at it now. But you just give me . . .
maybe ten minutes. I'm frightened to see what it
looks like. Can't we stop for a minute? Where
are we going . . . hang on, hang on . . .

CLINT   There's no need to panic, we're going to be
alright. There's no need to panic, we're going to
be alright. There's no need to panic, we're going
to be alright. There's no need to panic, we're
going to be alright. There's no need to panic,
we're going to be alright. There's no need to
panic, we're going to be alright. There's no need
to panic, we're going to be alright. There's no
need to panic, we're going to be alright. There's
no need to panic, we're going to be alright.
There's no need to . . . hang on, hang on . . .

BETTE   Right. Listen to me. Listen to me. Listen to me
you bastards. You're not fucking listening to me.
Shut the fuck up. Shut the fuck up. Will you
fucking listen? For fuck's sake. Fucking hell.
Shut the fuck up and listen to me for a fucking
minute. Shut up you bastards. You fucking
bastards. Fucking arseholes. Fucking wankers.

Dickheads. Shitheads. Will you shut the fuck up?
Let me talk let me talk let me talk let me talk let
me talk let me talk . . . hang on, hang on . . .

HENRY I feel like the nurse in *The Man Who Came To
Dinner*. Played by Mary Wickes. She says, "I am
not only walking out on this case, Mr Whiteside,
I am leaving the nursing profession. I became a
nurse because all my life, ever since I was a
little girl, I was filled with the idea of serving a
suffering humanity. After one month with you,
Mr Whiteside, I am going to work in a munitions
factory. From now on, anything I can do to help
exterminate the human race will fill me with the
greatest of . . ." Hang on, hang on . . .

(*Enter from the right,* CLINT, MARILYN, HENRY
and BETTE. CLINT *is carrying* MERYL *who is
unconscious. The lines continue to overlap so
that the conversation is a babble of voices and
each topic merges into the next one, improvising
around the following dialogue.*)

(A) Hang on/Hang on/Hang on/Hang on/Hang on a
minute/Hang on a moment/Hang on/Hang on/
Woah/Woah/Hang on/Hang on/Hang on/Hang
on . . .

(B) We're all talking at once/Everyone's talking at
the same time/We can't all talk at once/We can't
all speak at the same time/We can't fucking talk
like this/How can we talk like this?/Everyone's
talking at the same time for fuck's sake/You're
talking when I'm talking/You're talking when
I'm talking/We're all talking at the same time . . .

(C) Where are we going?/Does anyone know where
we're going?/We don't want to go too far from
the airplane/How will they find us if we're miles
away?/Does anybody know where the fuck we're
going?/What about here then?/I don't want to
walk any more/Can't we sit down?/Are we
staying here or what?/I think we'll be alright

here/Is this it then?/Is this it?/Where are we
going . . .

(D)   Quiet/Please be quiet/Shut the fuck up/Quiet/
        Quiet/Will you be quiet?/Shut up a minute/Shut
        up/You be quiet/You be quiet/Shut your fucking
        mouth/Shut up/Shut up/You shut up/Quiet/Quiet/
        Sssssh/Heh/Quiet . . .

(E)   You're talking when I'm talking/We're all
        talking at the same time/You're talking and he's
        talking and everyone's talking so how can you
        hear what I'm talking about?/We can't all talk at
        once/This is fucking ridiculous/I can't hear what
        you're saying/I can't hear what you're saying/
        We're all talking at the same fucking time/We're
        all talking at the same time . . .

(F)   Put her down/Why don't you put her down?/Go
        on then/Careful how you do it/Don't drop her/Go
        on, put her down/Don't drop her/Put her down/
        I'm putting her down/Don't drop her whatever
        you do/That's right/That's the way/Careful/
        Careful/Watch it/Don't drop her/I'm not going to
        drop her/Gently . . .

        (MERYL *is placed on her back.* MARILYN
        *rummages in the handbag which she has brought
        from the plane.*)

(G)   Don't crowd round/Let her breathe/Don't
        suffocate her/ Everyone stand back/Let the air
        get to her/Everyone stand back/Stand back come
        on/I am standing back/Fucking stand back/You
        stand back/You stand back/I am standing back/
        Everyone stand back/And you/Get back/And
        you . . .

(H)   Everyone calm down/Everyone calm down/Calm/
        Calm/Calm/I am calm/Everybody calm down/
        You calm down/Sssssssh/Let's calm down/Let's
        calm down/Let's calm down/You calm down/
        Everyone calm down/Calm/Calm/Calm/Calm/

Calm/Calm/I am calm/Everyone calm down/
Everyone/Calm/Calm down/Calm down . . .

(*Silence except for the rhythmic sound of the
waves. HENRY is looking around with suspicion
and anxiety. CLINT is looking manly. BETTE is
looking irritated by the inconvenience of events.
MARILYN is looking in her handbag which she has
brought from the plane. After a moment they
focus their attention on the unconscious body
except for MARILYN who remains preoccupied
with her handbag. The others look at MERYL . . .
with curiosity as much as concern.*)

HENRY   Is she dead?

(CLINT *is bending over the body . . . he stares at
it . . . prods it with his foot to see if it responds.*)

BETTE   Not like that! Have you never done a first aid
course?

(CLINT *withdraws reluctantly.* BETTE *bends over
the body . . . touches it to see if it's warm . . .
opens its eyelid and examines its eye . . . then
prods the body with her foot to see if it
responds.*)

HENRY   She dead or what?

BETTE   Sssh.

MARILYN   Oh God.

HENRY   What?

MARILYN   Can't find it.

HENRY   What?

MARILYN   Can't find my mirror. Hold this. Nothing's where
it should be. Everything's out of place.

(MARILYN *starts to give* HENRY *the contents of her
cluttered handbag to hold.*)

HENRY   Give us it when you find it. Have you got one?

MARILYN   I always carry a mirror.

HENRY   Hurry up.

MARILYN   I'm looking for it.

(MARILYN *searches her bag.* BETTE *continues to
feel* MERYL'S *neck and wrist and temples for a
pulse, sometimes bending close to* MERYL'S *mouth
to listen for breathing noises.* CLINT *makes
comments which make him feel useful. His
suggestions reflect rather than direct* BETTE'S
actions, and continue during the following.)

CLINT   Look for a pulse.

BETTE   What do you think I'm doing?

CLINT   Try the wrist. How about the neck? How about . . .
             try the wrist again, that's right.

HENRY   Is she dead or what?

BETTE   Sssssssssh!

HENRY   Are you sure you've done a first aid course?

CLINT   Try the other wrist. Try the . . . that's right,
             carry on like that.

(MARILYN *has found her powder compact. She is
looking at herself in the mirror and isn't pleased.
She adjusts her hair.*)

MARILYN   Oh God.

HENRY   Can I have that?

MARILYN   Don't look at me.

HENRY   Can I have the mirror *please*?

MARILYN   Get your own mirror.

HENRY   Can I have the mirror?

MARILYN   Will you not look at me PLEASE?

HENRY   I want the mirror.

MARILYN   You can borrow it when I've finished with it./
Can't say fairer than that.

HENRY   I want the mirror. Come on.

(HENRY *reaches for the mirror but* MARILYN *pulls it away . . . the tone of the conversation becomes increasingly strident.*)

MARILYN   Get off.

HENRY   Please.

MARILYN   This is mine.

HENRY   Can I have the mirror?

MARILYN   What do you want it for?

HENRY   I'll show you.

MARILYN   You can't have it.

HENRY   Give me the mirror.

MARILYN   No.

HENRY   I need it.

MARILYN   You can have it . . .

HENRY   Give it to me, then.

MARILYN   . . . when I've finished with it.

HENRY   That'll be too late.

MARILYN   For what?

HENRY   I'll show you.

MARILYN   Show me.

HENRY   Give me the mirror, then.

MARILYN   No.

HENRY   Won't be long.

MARILYN   What you going to do with it?

HENRY   I'll show you.

MARILYN   I want it back.

HENRY   You'll get it back.

(MARILYN *gives* HENRY *the powder compact containing the mirror. He holds the mirror over* MERYL'S *mouth.*)

HENRY   James Cagney.

BETTE   What about him?

HENRY   I saw him do this in a film.

CLINT   That's right, hold it over her mouth.

(HENRY *looks at* CLINT . . . *as if* CLINT *is stupid. After a moment* HENRY *examines the mirror.*)

MARILYN   Well?

(HENRY *places the mirror over* MERYL'S *mouth again.*)

MARILYN   How long does this take?

HENRY   Not long.

CLINT   Dig a grave, shall I?

HENRY   Hang on.

(HENRY *has another look at the mirror.*)

HENRY   James Cagney, he looks at the mirror, he looks/ up, and he says . . .

MARILYN   Never/mind James Cagney.

BETTE   Let me have a look.

HENRY   When James Cagney does it you don't get to see
          what's on the mirror. I think there's meant to be
          a mist. Can you see a mist?

BETTE   No.

HENRY   Last chance.

          (HENRY *places the mirror over* MERYL'S *mouth.*)

MARILYN   (*drily*) If she wakes up don't let her see in the
          mirror. If I woke up and saw I looked like that,
          I'd die.

BETTE   We're trying to help.

MARILYN   So am I.

BETTE   What are you doing?

MARILYN   It's my mirror.

BETTE   Have you anything useful to suggest?

MARILYN   Bit of powder on her face.

BETTE   I don't think so.

MARILYN   Put some colour in her cheeks.

BETTE   Oh yeah, it's a scene we're all familiar with. A
          terrible accident. People gather round. Someone
          fights her way through the crowd. Let me
          through, she says. Let me through, I'm a
          beautician.

          (*Meanwhile* HENRY *has examined the mirror and
          is showing it to* BETTE. BETTE *shakes her head.*
          HENRY *shakes his head.*)

CLINT   Dead?

HENRY   Dead.

CLINT   I'll dig a grave.

HENRY   That isn't necessary.

CLINT   Why not?

HENRY   Where are we?

CLINT   Don't know.

HENRY   How long are we here for?

CLINT   Don't know.

HENRY   How much food have we got?

CLINT   Food on the plane.

HENRY   How long will that last?

CLINT   Don't know.

HENRY   Exactly. Dig a hole if you like. And stick her in it so we don't have to look at her. But don't think of it as a grave. Think of it as a larder.

MARILYN   Meaning what?

HENRY   We might have to eat the body.

MARILYN   I'm not eating her.

HENRY   What are you going to eat?

MARILYN   I'm not eating her.

HENRY   Are you a vegetarian?

MARILYN   I'm not a cannibal.

HENRY   What are you going to eat?

MARILYN   Can I have my mirror back?

(MARILYN'S *mirror is returned to her. Meantime* BETTE *has continued the search for* MERYL'S *pulse.*)

BETTE Ssssssh. I've found a pulse.

HENRY (*surprised*) Where?

(BETTE *shows* HENRY *the location of* MERYL'S *pulse.* HENRY *feels the pulse.*)

CLINT I said try the wrist.

(CLINT'S *comment is ignored.*)

BETTE Well?

HENRY She's off the menu.

MARILYN Thank god for that.

(CLINT *starts to withdraw . . . eventually he exits left.*)

HENRY Now what?

BETTE Right.

(BETTE *puts* MERYL *brusquely into the recovery position. After she has done this she stands back.*)

MARILYN Is that it?

BETTE Yeah.

MARILYN Isn't there something else you can do?

BETTE Have you done a course?

MARILYN No.

BETTE What do you expect me to do, operate?

MARILYN How long was your course?

BETTE An afternoon.

MARILYN   Is that all you did?

BETTE   Wasn't a whole afternoon. Two o'clock till about half past four.

MARILYN   What else can you do?

BETTE   Nose bleeds. Splinters. Removing crash helmets. But she isn't wearing a fucking crash helmet.

            (*Beat.* MARILYN *looks out to sea.* HENRY *looks around warily.*)

MARILYN   How long before we're rescued?

BETTE   I don't know.

MARILYN   How long do you think?

BETTE   I don't know.

MARILYN   If you had to make a guess, how long would you say?

BETTE   I don't know.

MARILYN   What are we going to do?

BETTE   /I don't know.

MARILYN   You don't know.

HENRY   We must prepare for what's going to happen.

MARILYN   What's going to happen?

HENRY   Something nasty.

MARILYN   Like what?

HENRY   I can't say for sure.

MARILYN   How do we prepare?

HENRY   That depends on what we're preparing for.

MARILYN   And what's that?

HENRY   I just said, I'm not sure.

MARILYN   Then how do we prepare?

HENRY   That's the problem.

            (*Pause.* HENRY *is still looking around with foreboding.*)

BETTE   Have you done a course?

MARILYN   No.

BETTE   Well then.

            (*Pause.*)

MARILYN   Shouldn't someone have a look round?

HENRY   Yes, I think that's right.

BETTE   Who put you in charge?

HENRY   Me?

BETTE   Yeah.

HENRY   I'm not in charge.

BETTE   Talking as if you are.

HENRY   Me?

BETTE   Yeah.

HENRY   (*not sorry*) Sorry if I gave that impression.

BETTE   Don't start with me.

HENRY   I'm not.

            (*Pause.*)

HENRY   What do you want to do?

BETTE   I think we should have a look round.

HENRY   That's what I said.

BETTE   But first we vote on it.

HENRY   Okay.

BETTE   So it's fair.

HENRY   Okay.

BETTE   Those in favour say aye. Aye.

HENRY   Aye.

MARILYN   Aye.

BETTE   Come on then.

MARILYN   I'll stay here.

BETTE   Why?

MARILYN   Weak feet.

BETTE   Rubbish.

MARILYN   I have.

BETTE   How do you get about?

MARILYN   I only date men with cars.

BETTE   We're only going up that hill.

MARILYN   (*looks . . . and is shocked*) That hill over there!

BETTE   It's not that far.

MARILYN   I'd hold you back.

BETTE   Our ancestors travelled hundreds of miles on foot.

MARILYN   That was two million years ago when we were hunter-gatherers. But we're not hunter-gatherers any more. We're shoppers. My idea of a marathon: walking from Boots to C&A, realising

I've forgotten the deodorant, and having to walk back to Boots.

BETTE   Come on.

MARILYN   Wouldn't be fair to you.

(CLINT *enters from the left*.)

CLINT   Alright, I'm back. Don't worry about a thing. I'll look after us. I'll make sure we're alright. Leave it to me. I'll sort it out. (CLINT *looks at* MERYL.) How is she now?

BETTE   What's it look like?

CLINT   I thought you knew first aid.

BETTE   Oh, fuck off.

CLINT   How are you feeling?

BETTE   Fine.

CLINT   Don't hold them back.

BETTE   What?

CLINT   Tears.

BETTE   We've had a vote and decided to explore the area.

CLINT   Yeah, I've just done that.

BETTE   Where've you been?

CLINT   Top of the hill. Sea for miles in every direction.

BETTE   What can you see?

CLINT   No, that's what I saw. The sea.

MARILYN   If there's sea in every/direction . . .

BETTE   An island.

CLINT   Over there, miles of sea. Over there, miles of sea. Over there, miles of sea. Over there, miles of trees.

MARILYN   Beyond the trees?

CLINT   The sea.

MARILYN   Villages?

CLINT   None.

MARILYN   Buildings?

CLINT   None.

MARILYN   People?

CLINT   None.

MARILYN   Phone boxes?

CLINT   /None.

MARILYN   None.

HENRY   Food? Apples, oranges, apricots, peaches, pears, bananas, pineapples, edible berries?

CLINT   None.

HENRY   Can you tell the difference between edible berries and inedible berries?

CLINT   Yes, but only after I've eaten them.

HENRY   You can't?

CLINT   No, I can't.

HENRY   So how do you know they weren't edible?

CLINT   Wasn't a problem. There were no berries of any kind.

BETTE   Nothing to eat?

CLINT   All I saw was sea and trees.

BETTE	What kind of trees?
CLINT	(*won't admit he doesn't know*) All sorts.
BETTE	Because there are certain kinds of leaves we can eat.
MARILYN	The most exotic thing I've eaten in my life is Alpen. Tropical variety, different kinds of nuts/ in it.
BETTE	So?
MARILYN	I didn't like that. No way I can eat leaves.
BETTE	And I read something in the *Guardian* about people who survived by sucking fluid from the spinal cavities of fish.
MARILYN	(*not in a million years*) Oh yeah?
HENRY	Some trees have a sap you can drink.
MARILYN	Oh yeah?
HENRY	Saw it in a film.
MARILYN	I can't drink sap. I don't like Ribena. And sucking fish? (*Pulls face . . . shakes head.*) Weak stomach.
	(*Pause.* CLINT *exits right during the following.*)
HENRY	And we need to build shelters for the night.
BETTE	You still think you're in charge, don't you?
HENRY	(*quoting something*) I've met a lot of hard-boiled eggs in my life, but you, you're twenty minutes.
BETTE	Vote on it.
HENRY	Those in favour say aye. Aye.
BETTE	Aye.
MARILYN	Aye don't think we'll be here tonight.

HENRY   We will.

MARILYN   Tonight? Nahhhhh. Search parties are looking for
            us.

HENRY   Won't find us for a while.

MARILYN   When will they find us?

HENRY   Days.

MARILYN   Days!

HENRY   If we're lucky.

MARILYN   You think we'll be here tonight?

            (*In the background* CLINT *enters from the right,
            crosses the stage and exits left. He is carrying
            supplies from the airplane.*)

BETTE   So we go to the plane . . .

HENRY   Take what we need . . .

BETTE   Carry it over there . . .

HENRY   Make a camp . . .

BETTE   Somewhere in the trees . . .

HENRY   Edge of the beach . . .

BETTE   Those in favour say aye. Aye.

HENRY   Aye.

MARILYN   Aye don't want to carry anything.

BETTE   You won't have to carry much.

MARILYN   How much?

BETTE   Your fair share.

MARILYN   Sounds like a lot to me.

BETTE   Where will you sleep tonight?

MARILYN   In the plane.

BETTE   (*as if remembering*) With all the dead bodies?
             Blood oozing and dripping on to the ruptured
             metal?

HENRY   Stench of death in your nose.

BETTE   People's brains leaking on to their seats.

             (*Pause.*)

MARILYN   Alright. You can't expect me to carry much. I've
             got weak arms.

             (*They exit right, leaving* MERYL *where she is.*
             HENRY *is looking around warily.*)

Scene Three

The beach. It becomes darker as evening approaches. MERYL
remains inert.

HENRY *enters from the right carrying a cumbersome load. He
crosses the stage and exits left.* BETTE *enters from the right
carrying a cumbersome load. She crosses the stage and exits
left.* MARILYN *enters from the right carrying something light,
such as two cushions and a copy of 'Cosmopolitan'. She looks
out to sea. She arranges one of the cushions on the beach and
sits on it. She produces her compact and begins to apply
powder to* MERYL'S *face.* HENRY *enters from the left with a
slight limp. He sits on the other cushion.*

HENRY   Ugh.

MARILYN   I'm not used to it, sorry.

HENRY   Ugh.

MARILYN   My idea of heavy is a glass of Martini with two
             lumps of ice. Put a slice of lemon in it as well
             and the veins stand out on my arms.

HENRY   Ugh, my leg.

MARILYN   She hasn't got a bad face. But she's done nothing
             with it.

HENRY   It got a knock when we crashed.

MARILYN   I'm going to transform her.

HENRY   Then I just tripped over a tree stump.

MARILYN   Shock of her life when she wakes up. She'll
             think she's died and gone to heaven.

HENRY   Stubbed my toe.

MARILYN   I was hoping they'd be here by now.

HENRY   Who?

MARILYN   Rescue party.

HENRY   I told you.

             (MARILYN *is looking out to sea.*)

MARILYN   What's that over there?

HENRY   Nothing.

             (BETTE *enters with a blanket.*)

BETTE   What's up with you?

HENRY   Leg. It got a knock when we crashed. Then I just
             tripped over a tree stump. Stubbed my toe.

BETTE   And you?

MARILYN   I've been looking after her.

             (BETTE *places a blanket over* MERYL.)

BETTE   How is she?

MARILYN   Not bad. Nice eyebrows. Her bone structure is
             functional rather than decorative. She's not a

magazine cover. She's not *Vogue*. But she's not *Horse and Hound*.

(CLINT *enters from the left.*)

BETTE   How is she in herself?

MARILYN   Hard to say.

BETTE   Don't mess with her.

MARILYN   What do you mean, mess?

CLINT   What's wrong with you lot?

HENRY   It's my leg. It got a knock when we crashed. Then I just tripped over a tree stump. I've got a stubbed toe.

CLINT   What kind of a toe?

HENRY   Stubbed.

CLINT   What are you sitting on?

HENRY   Cushion.

CLINT   A what?

HENRY   A cushion.

MARILYN   I gave it to him.

HENRY   She gave it to me.

MARILYN   I've got one as well.

CLINT   Listen. Shelters. I can make one big one that we share or I can make separate ones. What do you prefer?

BETTE   Separate.

HENRY   Separate.

MARILYN   Separate.

BETTE   You got enough?

CLINT   Plenty of blankets. Canopy, blanket.
           Groundsheet, blanket. Pillow, blanket rolled up.
           Problem is, tying the canopy to the trees. I
           thought, rope.

BETTE   Haven't got any rope.

CLINT   Correct. I thought, cord.

BETTE   Haven't got any cord.

CLINT   Correct. I thought,/the wiring in the aeroplane.

BETTE   The wiring in the aeroplane.

CLINT   Get in the cockpit, rip out the instrument panel,
           all the wire we need.

BETTE   Come on then.

CLINT   Won't be easy.

BETTE   I know.

CLINT   Needs a bit of strength.

BETTE   I know.

CLINT   I admire your spirit.

BETTE   What are you saying?

CLINT   Man's job.

HENRY   (*feeling his toe*) Ugggggggggh.

BETTE   What about his leg?

CLINT   He's man enough.

           (HENRY *rises unhappily.*)

HENRY   Ugh.

CLINT   Good man.

HENRY   Ugggh.

BETTE	Does it hurt?
HENRY	There's a scene in *Lawrence of Arabia* — 1962. David Lean film. Peter O'Toole, Alec Guinness . . . anyway — there's this bit where Lawrence of Arabia holds his hand over the flame of a match and doesn't flinch. And someone says to him, "does it hurt?" "Yes," says Lawrence of Arabia, "the secret is not minding that it hurts."

(HENRY *winces as he walks off*.)

CLINT	Come on.
HENRY	Alright.
CLINT	Getting dark.

(CLINT *and* HENRY *exit right*. MARILYN *settles on her cushion*.)

MARILYN	See you then! Good luck! Rather you than me.
BETTE	Come on.
MARILYN	What/?
BETTE	Get up.
MARILYN	I've just got comfy.
BETTE	We need logs for a fire.
MARILYN	Heavy logs?
BETTE	Like feathers.
MARILYN	I can't leave her alone.
BETTE	Yes you can.

(MARILYN *is looking out to sea*.)

MARILYN	Look. A ship! Coming this way. Knew they'd find us. Yes! Yes! Yes!

BETTE   Nothing there.

MARILYN   What's that over there?

BETTE   Where?

           (MARILYN *points . . . peers . . . stops pointing.*)

MARILYN   Could have sworn there was something.

BETTE   You're an optimist, aren't you?

MARILYN   I am.

BETTE   Heard the one about the optimist and the
           pessimist?

MARILYN   Go on.

BETTE   There's a shipwreck. Two survivors are floating
           in the sea. One's an optimist, one's a pessimist.
           They both drown.

MARILYN   Is that it?

BETTE   We need logs.

MARILYN   How heavy?

BETTE   Feathers.

MARILYN   Ah well then.

           (MARILYN *and* BETTE *exit left with the cushions
           and 'Cosmopolitan'. The beach becomes darker
           as night approaches.* CLINT *and* HENRY *enter from
           the right clutching wire of various lengths.*
           HENRY *still has a slight limp. They cross the
           stage and exit left. It is night.*)

                    Scene Four

The beach. It is morning. MERYL *is inert.* MARILYN *enters from
the left. She stares at the empty sea.* HENRY *enters from the
left.*

HENRY   Anything?

MARILYN   Nothing.

HENRY   I knew it.

MARILYN   Can you see anything?

HENRY   No.

MARILYN   I can't.

HENRY   Do you like the sea?

MARILYN   Yeah, I like the sea. At Blackpool. Brighton. Bridlington. Don't like this sea. There are no amenities. More like Southport, this. See over there? (*She points out to sea.*)

HENRY   Yeah.

MARILYN   What is that?

HENRY   Nothing.

MARILYN   No, next to that, further along.

HENRY   Nothing.

(MARILYN *sighs.*)

HENRY   It's the hope I can't stand, not the despair. John Cleese says that in a film.

(CLINT *enters from the left.*)

CLINT   Morning.

HENRY   Morning.

CLINT   Morning.

MARILYN   Hello.

CLINT   No boats?

MARILYN   No.

CLINT   No planes?

MARILYN   No.

            (CLINT *is standing behind* MARILYN *and touching her 'comfortingly'*.)

CLINT   No helicopters?

MARILYN   No.

CLINT   No ships?

MARILYN   No.

CLINT   No matter.

            (*Now his whole body is against hers and his manner indicates the presence of feelings other than sympathy.* HENRY *watches.* BETTE *enters from the left. A general exchange of good mornings.*)

ALL   Morning/Good morning/Good morning/Morning.

HENRY   Saw a film about a plane that crashed in the Amazon. Wasn't found for weeks.

MARILYN   Where was it flying?

HENRY   Mexico to Bermuda, somewhere like that.

MARILYN   Not Gatwick to Majorca?

HENRY   No.

MARILYN   Bermuda Triangle I've heard of. Haven't heard of the Majorca Triangle.

            (*This brings an ingratiating laugh from* CLINT.)

HENRY   We're not near Majorca.

MARILYN   Where are we, the Amazon?

(*Another sycophantic laugh from* CLINT . . . *and more touching.*)

HENRY   Possibly.

MARILYN   Bit of a long way round. Gatwick to Majorca via the Amazon. Pilot used to be a taxi driver — still thought he was being paid by the mile. Is that what you think?

BETTE   He means we're miles off course. Vicious storm like that. /Blew us all over the place. Could be anywhere.

MARILYN   Is that what you mean?

HENRY   Not really.

(HENRY *is looking around warily.*)

MARILYN   You'd think they'd've found us by now.

HENRY   They won't find us.

MARILYN   What, ever?

HENRY   Not yet.

MARILYN   Why not?

HENRY   I don't want to say.

MARILYN   Where do you think we are?

HENRY   You wouldn't believe me if I told you.

MARILYN   What do you keep looking round for?

HENRY   You wouldn't believe me/if I told you.

MARILYN   If you told me.

(*Pause.*)

MARILYN   Is that a ship over there?

HENRY   No.

(CLINT *has been touching* MARILYN *all this time.*
MARILYN *disengages abruptly.*)

MARILYN   Heh.

CLINT   Sorry.

MARILYN   Is that what I think it is?

CLINT   Yeah.

MARILYN   (*at-a-time-like-this*) Urrrrh.

CLINT   Sorry.

MARILYN   I wondered what it was.

CLINT   It's something I have no control over.

MARILYN   Can't you stop it?

CLINT   No.

MARILYN   At a time like this.

CLINT   It happens.

MARILYN   I don't believe you can't control it.

CLINT   Can't stop it, nothing I can do, you know, ask
            him.

MARILYN   Is this true?

HENRY   When they were making the film *Conspirator*,
            the actor kissing Elizabeth Taylor told the
            cameraman to film him only from the waist up.

MARILYN   But in a life-and-death situation like this.

HENRY   Makes no difference. In a 1948 film called *Red
            River* Montgomery Clift was being attacked by
            Indians. He wasn't bothered about the Indians.
            I'll tell you what Montgomery Clift was bothered
            about. Her name was Joanne Dru. Know what I
            mean?

CLINT   Mind of its own.

MARILYN   Bloody hell.

CLINT   Sorry.

BETTE   And you've been looking at my breasts.

CLINT   Me?

BETTE   I've seen you.

CLINT   Sorry.

               (*Pause. They look out to sea.*)

BETTE   We have to get on together.

CLINT   Yeah.

BETTE   Our survival depends on it.

MARILYN   Get on with anyone, me.

BETTE   Doesn't matter that we're strangers.

HENRY   Practically all the people I know were strangers when I met them. That's a line from a 1946 film called *The Blue Dahlia*. Alan Ladd, Veronica Lake. Written by Raymond Chandler.

MARILYN   Why do you go on about films?

HENRY   You can learn a lot from films.

MARILYN   Like what?

HENRY   You wouldn't believe me if I told you.

MARILYN   I'm sick of you saying that. Tell me.

HENRY   I could tell you something that would shatter the illusions on which your life is based.

MARILYN   Go on then.

HENRY   Prepare for a shock.

MARILYN   Get on with it.

HENRY   The fact is . . . we're all characters in a film.

MARILYN   Oh yeah?

HENRY   I've said enough.

MARILYN   And why haven't we been found, do you think?

HENRY   Could be one of a number of reasons.

MARILYN   Such as?

HENRY   A time warp.

MARILYN   A what?

HENRY   Have you seen *Planet of the Apes*?

MARILYN   Oh I see, a time warp.

HENRY   It's a possibility.

MARILYN   Like in *Planet of the Apes*.

HENRY   Yes.

MARILYN   Why didn't I think of that?

HENRY   I said you wouldn't believe me.

           (*Pause.*)

BETTE   So don't look at my breasts again, alright?

CLINT   Yeah.

BETTE   This is an opportunity. To live in a community
           that's egalitarian. We can discard the prejudices
           of our upbringing and behave without
           discrimination against any person on the grounds
           of, for example, gender. Can't we?

CLINT   Yeah.

MARILYN   What's for breakfast?

BETTE	The sort of thing I mean — looking at breasts. Banned. No more.
CLINT	Alright.
BETTE	And then we'll all get along fine.
HENRY	New names.
MARILYN	Are we having breakfast?
HENRY	I'd like to be called Henry.
BETTE	Okay.
HENRY	I've always wanted to be called Henry.
BETTE	Okay.
HENRY	After Henry Fonda.
BETTE	Okay.
MARILYN	There's an actress people say I look like.
HENRY	Which actress?
MARILYN	Can't you tell?
HENRY	Is she well known?
MARILYN	Yes.
HENRY	Is it Raquel out of *Coronation Street*?
MARILYN	No.
HENRY	Just round the eyes you look a bit like her.
MARILYN	You're not looking.
HENRY	I am. Who is it?
MARILYN	I'm telling you what people have said.
HENRY	An actress?

MARILYN   Yes.

HENRY   Tell me her first name.

MARILYN   Marilyn.

HENRY   Monroe?

MARILYN   More than one person has remarked on the
            resemblance.

HENRY   Marilyn Monroe?

MARILYN   Can you see it now?

HENRY   You're not physically identical though are you?

MARILYN   Someone said it was a sexual charisma we had in
            common.

CLINT   I can see it.

HENRY   Is there an actor you like?

CLINT   Clint Eastwood.

HENRY   What about you?

BETTE   Who is there? In Hollywood women are either in
            bed or dead. If an actress is vertical there's a
            man at her side so that she can lean on him when
            she needs to because of the weakness of her sex,
            and if she's horizontal there's a man at her side
            so that he can lean on her when he needs to
            because of the weakness of his sex. Name me an
            independent actress.

HENRY   Katharine Hepburn. Glenn Close. Jodie Foster.
            Sigourney Weaver.

BETTE   Bette Davis.

HENRY   Marilyn Monroe, Clint Eastwood, Bette Davis,
            Henry Fonda. Right then.

MARILYN   Shall we have breakfast?

BETTE　　　Who was snoring last night?

MARILYN　Yeah, who was that?

CLINT　　I didn't hear anything.

HENRY　　Did anyone hear strange noises?

MARILYN　What kind of noises?

HENRY　　Animal noises.

MARILYN　No.

HENRY　　We must be careful. Something terrible is going to happen.

MARILYN　Why do you say that?

HENRY　　That's what always happens in films.

MARILYN　You're mad, aren't you?

HENRY　　That's what they said about Richard Carlson.

MARILYN　Richard who?

HENRY　　Have you seen a 1953 film called *It Came From Outer Space*?

MARILYN　Don't think I have.

HENRY　　He was in that.

MARILYN　Was he good?

HENRY　　He was the one who knew what was going on but no one believed him.

MARILYN　He wasn't mad, then?

HENRY　　He was a genius. In one scene Charles Drake says to him, "This town doesn't understand geniuses. You frighten them, and what frightens them they don't like." And Richard Carlson makes this speech about the imagination — the "willingness to believe there are things we don't understand . . ."

MARILYN   Sounds a good film. What's it called?

HENRY   *It Came From Outer Space.*

MARILYN   I'll keep an eye out for that one.

           (*They start to exit towards breakfast.*)

HENRY   (*to* BETTE) My favourite Bette Davis line was about an actress . . . "she's the original good time that was had by all." I can tell you every film she was in, Bette Davis. *All About Eve . . .* do you want it chronologically or alphabetically?

           (HENRY'S *voice trails away as he and* BETTE *exit right.*)

CLINT   You're having breakfast, are you?

MARILYN   We could go somewhere and fuck.

CLINT   Okay.

           (MARILYN *and* CLINT *exit left. After a moment* MERYL *wakes up. She looks around and exits right with the blanket. Night falls.*)

Scene Five

The next day. The sun is intense. BETTE *and* MARILYN *enter from opposite sides of the beach.*

MARILYN   Miles I've walked.

BETTE   Where've you looked?

MARILYN   Phhhf.

           (MARILYN *waves a hand to suggest she has searched half the island.*)

BETTE   Have you seen her?

MARILYN   No I haven't.

BETTE   Where is she?

MARILYN   She can die as far as I'm concerned.

              (CLINT *enters wearing a Clint Eastwood hat.*
              BETTE *stares at it disdainfully.*)

BETTE   What have you got on your head?

CLINT   Hat.

BETTE   From?

CLINT   One of the passengers.

BETTE   You took it off a dead person?

CLINT   No use to him, is it?

BETTE   I thought you were searching the plane.

CLINT   Done it.

BETTE   And?

CLINT   Found this hat. Bit of blood on it. Makes it more
              authentic as a cowboy hat. Found another hat
              with KISS ME QUICK on the front but it's not
              really Clint Eastwood. /Clint doesn't ride into
              Dodge City with KISS ME QUICK on his hat.

BETTE   Have you looked in the trees over there?

MARILYN   Which ones? Errrr . . .

BETTE   Don't you know?

MARILYN   I probably have.

CLINT   I'll have a look. Leave it to me. Don't you
              worry.

              (CLINT *exits left.*)

MARILYN   They're starting to smell.

BETTE   What are?

MARILYN   The people on the plane.

BETTE   It's the heat. You have to expect a bit of a smell.
           I'll look over here. Will you look over there?

MARILYN   Yes.

BETTE   Promise.

MARILYN   Yes.

           (BETTE *exits right.* MARILYN *stays where she is
           and gazes towards the distant trees.*)

MARILYN   No, she's not over there.

           (MARILYN *looks out to sea.* HENRY *enters from the
           left. He looks at* MARILYN. MARILYN *ignores him.*)

HENRY   It would spoil the plot if we were rescued now.
           Have you seen *The Poseidon Adventure*?

MARILYN   About thirty times. Every Christmas they put it
           on.

HENRY   They weren't rescued in scene five, were they?

MARILYN   But that was a film.

HENRY   So is this.

MARILYN   I can feel it though.

HENRY   What?

MARILYN   Help is just around the corner.

HENRY   That's the thing about the sea — it's got no
           corners. You can see for miles. You can see how
           alone you are.

MARILYN   There's something out there. Just can't see it yet.

HENRY   I believe in logic and the power of reason. Ever
            since I saw Henry Fonda in *Twelve Angry Men*.
            Brilliant film. Have you seen that?

MARILYN   I said I'd look over there.

HENRY   Okay.

MARILYN   What will you do?

HENRY   I'll come with you.

MARILYN   Right.

HENRY   There's nobody like Henry Fonda these days.
            Rocky, Rambo and Robocop — they're nothing
            compared to Henry Fonda. There wouldn't have
            been a nightmare on Elm Street if Henry Fonda
            had been around. He would have had them all
            sitting round a table, talking things over.

            (MARILYN *and* HENRY *exit left.* CLINT *enters left
            and exits right.* MERYL *enters right and exits left.*
            MARILYN *enters from the left.* BETTE *enters from
            the right.*)

BETTE   I thought Henry was with you.

MARILYN   He was.

BETTE   What happened to him?

MARILYN   I looked round and he wasn't there.

BETTE   On purpose?

MARILYN   He was going on and on about some film with
            Henry Fonda in it. Takes longer to hear him
            describe a film than it does to watch it.

BETTE   So have we lost him as well?

MARILYN   He's a man, isn't he? It means he knows about
            jungle survival, stuff like that. If he read the
            right comics as a boy he'll know how to skin

rabbits with his teeth. My brother used to read comics like that. He knew where to put your hands on someone's head if you wanted to break their neck. He used to try it on me.

BETTE   Wasn't that dangerous?

MARILYN   He was only ten.

BETTE   What's he like now?

MARILYN   Okay. He gets parole in three years. He's a nice fella.

BETTE   Two people we've lost now.

MARILYN   The only number I care about is Number One.

BETTE   Don't you care about other people?

MARILYN   (*surprised*) Do you?

BETTE   Women.

MARILYN   You know what you are?

BETTE   What?

MARILYN   You're a lying git. List of priorities: number one?

BETTE   Me.

MARILYN   That's right.

BETTE   Number two, women.

MARILYN   Then men?

BETTE   No. Then cats and dogs, rabbits, dolphins, elephants, whales. Then the rest of the animal kingdom. Except snakes. Then the world of Nature: lakes, streams, waterfalls, Yorkshire, Scottish Highlands, Lake District, Peak District, South Downs. Then the rest of the physical universe. Then snakes. Then men.

(CLINT *enters from the right. He has something behind his back.*)

Have you seen her?

CLINT   No.

BETTE   What have you got behind your back?

CLINT   Something.

BETTE   Thought you were searching over there.

CLINT   Ages ago. Came back. Had another look round the plane. Found this.

(*From behind his back* CLINT *produces a gun.*)

MARILYN   Is it a real one?

CLINT   Yup.

MARILYN   Let's have a look then.

CLINT   You can't.

MARILYN   Why not?

CLINT   It's loaded.

MARILYN   Take the bullets out.

CLINT   They're not bullets. It's a flare gun.

MARILYN   Oh it's not dangerous then.

CLINT   It is.

MARILYN   Can't kill anything.

CLINT   It could. If you hit someone in the right place. In the heart or smack between the eyes.

BETTE   What do you want a gun for?

CLINT   Clint Eastwood does what he wants. It goes with the hat.

BETTE   I mean it.

CLINT   Got the hat. Got the gun. All I need now is the horse.

BETTE   And someone to kill.

            (HENRY *enters from the left*.)

CLINT   It's well balanced. Medium calibre. It's a nice piece.

BETTE   How do you know about guns?

CLINT   *Weapons of War*.

BETTE   What's that?

CLINT   It's an encyclopedia published in weekly parts.

BETTE   Was issue two free with issue one?

CLINT   That's right.

BETTE   And you get a free binder?

CLINT   That's right.

BETTE   I've always wondered who bought those things.

HENRY   Where did you go?

MARILYN   I looked round and you'd vanished.

HENRY   I shouted for you.

MARILYN   Oh was that you?

HENRY   Did you hear me shouting or not?

MARILYN   No.

HENRY   (*looking at the gun*) What's that?

CLINT   'S alright, init?

BETTE   Have you seen her?

HENRY   Who? Meryl? No.

BETTE   Who's Meryl?

HENRY   Meryl Streep.

BETTE   Why have you called her/Meryl Streep?

HENRY   Because I like Meryl Streep.

BETTE   Where is she?

HENRY   I've been thinking about all the films I've seen
           and what might have happened to her. It's
           possible that she's here but she's invisible.

           (HENRY *is feeling the air.* MERYL *enters from the
           left.*)

MARILYN   No, here she is.

HENRY   Stand back everyone. Watch her. Watch her.

BETTE   What's the matter?

HENRY   I'm making sure, that's all.

BETTE   What?

HENRY   Have you seen *Invasion of the Body Snatchers*?

BETTE   She looks alright.

HENRY   That's exactly what they want you to think.

BETTE   Don't be stupid.

HENRY   Careful, she might have strange powers.

           (*They approach* MERYL *tentatively.*)

HENRY   Stand back!

BETTE   What's the matter?

HENRY   She could be possessed by evil forces.

BETTE   Let me talk to her.

HENRY   No. You don't know what you're dealing with. Leave this to me. (*He takes one tentative step forward.*) See how hostile she looks.

BETTE   Are you surprised?

HENRY   It's also possible she's an android, an exact replica of the human form. It's possible her face is a mask.

BETTE   You'll frighten her.

HENRY   Something's definitely wrong. I don't like it.

ALL   Henry!/Calm down/Henry.

HENRY   You can't say I didn't warn you. Afterwards, when it's too late, you can't say I didn't warn you.

(BETTE *is approaching* MERYL.)

HENRY   Be very careful.

BETTE   No, it's alright.

HENRY   Watch her! Watch her!

BETTE   (*to* MERYL) Come on. You're safe now. You're with us.

(BETTE *and* CLINT *silently advance towards* MERYL. *These three freeze in position. It gets darker.* MARILYN *is picking at a loose thread on her clothing.*)

HENRY   You try to help people . . . they don't listen.

MARILYN   (*absently*) Nn?

HENRY   I had a dream last night. Do you remember that great bit in *Spartacus*? Where the emperor says he will spare the life of all the slaves if they identify Spartacus. So Kirk Douglas stands up to identify himself. But as he stands up, Tony

Curtis stands up as well, and he shouts out, "I'm
Spartacus!" Then someone else stands up and
shouts, "I'm Spartacus!" Then all the slaves are
standing up and shouting, "I'm Spartacus! I'm
Spartacus! I'm Spartacus!"

(*Beat.*)

That's what my dream was about. Only it wasn't
Kirk Douglas. It was me. When the emperor said
he'd spare the life of all the slaves if they
identified Spartacus, I was thinking, shall I stand
up or not? But while I was thinking about it,
Tony Curtis stood up. And he shouted out, "He's
Spartacus!" Then someone else stood up and
shouted out, "He's Spartacus!" Soon all the
slaves were standing up, pointing at me, shouting
"He's Spartacus! He's Spartacus! He's
Spartacus!"

Scene Six

*The beach. The lighting change signifies that some time has
passed. It is later in the day.* BETTE, HENRY, MARILYN *and*
CLINT *have discovered that* MERYL *has lost her memory.* CLINT
is practising twirling the gun.

BETTE   We know from phrenology that different parts of
             the brain have distinct functions. Her brain has
             sustained injuries at specific points of impact so
             that the damage is significant but localised.

CLINT   Bang on the head. Lost her memory.

MARILYN   So she's not an alien?

HENRY   There are no signs yet.

MARILYN   What kind of signs?

HENRY   Objects moving strangely. Or she might get
             bigger and bigger until she's as big as the lead
             character in *The Attack of the Fifty Foot Woman*.

Depends whether she's been secretly exposed to radiation.

BETTE   That's ridiculous.

HENRY   It's what happened to *The Incredible Shrinking Man*. He got smaller and smaller.

             (MERYL *has been looking at* CLINT *twirling the gun.*)

CLINT   What's she staring at?

BETTE   Social skills are a function of learnt behaviour. She's forgotten all that.

CLINT   I'll remind her. Fuck off.

BETTE   Don't swear at her.

CLINT   It's a learning experience for her. And if she stares again she'll get a learning experience round the ear.

BETTE   Will you get rid of that gun?

             (CLINT *exits manfully left with the gun, still twirling. Pause. The others look at* MERYL *who has a small, vacant smile.*)

BETTE   It's almost as if she's a child.

MARILYN   Seems quite happy.

HENRY   Happiness is a failure to understand how bad things are. Bliss is ignorance.

MARILYN   What's up with you?

HENRY   I hate kids. Kids at school made fun of me because I knew we were all characters in a film and they didn't. The only kid I like is the Sundance Kid.

BETTE   Keeping an eye on her — we'll have to take turns.

HENRY   I'll go last.

(HENRY *exits.*)

Scene Seven

Later. The beach. It is darker. BETTE *is playing with* MERYL.
MARILYN *is anxious.*

MARILYN   Can I ask you something?

BETTE   What?

MARILYN   Do you like rings?

BETTE   My mother used to say that marriage was about
            three rings,/engagement ring, wedding ring and
            suffering.

MARILYN   Engagement ring, wedding ring and suffering.
            Yeah, it's a good one, that. Do you like rings?

BETTE   I think fashion is a form of slavery. We deceive
            ourselves that what we wear is an expression of
            our freedom, when really it's a poor substitute
            for more fundamental freedoms we're denied.
            We're too busy admiring our own clothes to
            notice that we're living in a cage.

MARILYN   Do you like rings or not?

BETTE   Oh yes I do.

MARILYN   Do you like mine?

(MARILYN *shows* BETTE *her rings.*)

MARILYN   They're eternity rings from ex-boyfriends. I'm
            like a tree — the older I get, the more rings I
            have.

BETTE   Nice.

MARILYN   There was a woman on the plane. Fat woman
            near me. She had a beautiful ring. I noticed it
            when she sat down.

BETTE   And?

MARILYN   Today I went on board the plane to have another
            look. Just to have a look, like.

BETTE   And?

MARILYN   Not there any more.

BETTE   The ring?

MARILYN   The woman.

BETTE   Is this a joke?

MARILYN   No.

BETTE   Show me.

            (BETTE, MARILYN *and* MERYL *exit right.*)

Scene Eight

Later. The beach. Everyone enters at once.

BETTE   Tall man, broken nose, bald head. He was with a
            woman, greasy hair, glasses. They were sitting in
            front of me. They're not there any more.

MARILYN   Near me there was a family. The mother, the
            father, two daughters. The mother is still there.
            The father isn't. The two daughters aren't.

BETTE   In a seat near me there was an old woman, fur
            coat and a wig. Nothing remains except one of
            her hands. There's a jagged wound where it was
            separated from the arm. Either it was torn off or
            it was bitten off.

HENRY   Now do you believe me?

MARILYN   What do you think it is?

HENRY   Could be anything. *The Monster That Challenged the World*, it was a giant snail. *It Came From Beneath the Sea*, it was a giant octopus. *The Attack of the Crab Monsters*, it was crab monsters. *The Beginning of the End*, it was grasshoppers.

MARILYN   No.

HENRY   I know you find it hard to believe. Think of it like this. The first people to see a giant snail were no more frightened than the first people to see an elephant. Our world is full of grotesque things, it's only because they're familiar that they don't seem grotesque. That's why the unknown must be taken seriously — because it can't be any more implausible than the known.

            (*During that speech people have started to show doubt and fear.*)

ALL   No/Rubbish/Monster?/Well whatever it is/Bloody hell/Shit/Fuck/Fucking hell/Oh God/Keep calm/ No need to panic/Fucking hell/Whatever it is/ Shit/Oh God . . .

MARILYN   What do we do?

CLINT   Kill it.

ALL   Yeah, kill it/Kill the bastard/Kill it/Kill it/Yeah, go on/Fucking kill it . . .

BETTE   Everyone keep/together.

MARILYN   Keep/together everyone.

CLINT   Is everyone here?

ALL   Keep together/Move in/Come on/Everyone keep together . . .

            (BETTE, MARILYN, HENRY, MERYL *and* CLINT *exit left together.*)

Scene Nine

The beach. Towards dusk. Fog has seeped in from the sea.
HENRY, BETTE, MARILYN, MERYL *and* CLINT *enter in a huddle.*
HENRY *is feeling crowded in.*

BETTE   We have to walk everywhere together.

HENRY   I know.

CLINT   Safer that way.

MARILYN   Can't be too careful.

HENRY   But do we have to be so close?

BETTE   Yes we do.

CLINT   Safer that way.

MARILYN   Can't be too careful.

            (HENRY *continues to walk across the beach. The
            others follow close behind.* HENRY *stops.*)

HENRY   Footprint.

MARILYN   It's enormous.

CLINT   It's wild and savage. You can tell because it
            doesn't wear shoes.

BETTE   The British built an empire on that principle.
            Everything that wasn't wearing shoes was
            educated into civilised values, or killed.

ALL   Kill the bastard/Kill it/Kill it/Yeah, kill it/
            Fucking kill it.

MARILYN   How we going to kill that?

BETTE   We've got the gun.

CLINT   I forgot the gun.

ALL	You what?/Where is it?/Stupid bastard!
CLINT	Alright.
HENRY	I've seen all the Clint Eastwood movies. He never does that.
CLINT	Sorry.

(CLINT *exits left. The others exit right, keeping close together*.)

ALL	Stupid bastard/Keep together/Move in/Come nearer/Wanker/Everyone keep together/Dickhead . . .

Scene Ten

The beach. Off stage there is a ferocious roar and screaming. Dramatic B-Movie music.

CLINT *enters from the left in Clint Eastwood style with his hat and the gun. He crosses the beach and exits right. The others enter from the right, walking backwards fearfully from the monster which is advancing towards them. We hear the firing of the gun. The monster is dead. There is general relief. Everyone exits.* BETTE *and* CLINT *enter. They stroll along the beach.*

BETTE	Are you sure it's dead?
CLINT	Oh yeah.
BETTE	Well done.
CLINT	Someone had to do it.
BETTE	I would have done it.
CLINT	No, you couldn't.
BETTE	Where do you get your ideas from?
CLINT	Wasn't a job for a woman.

BETTE   What kind of woman was your mother?

CLINT   Good cook.

BETTE   Women don't live in kitchens any more. The
             only time I've been tied to a sink I had to draw
             the curtains because there was a naked Italian
             kneeling on the draining board.

CLINT   My mother liked the kitchen.

BETTE   All women are not/like your mother.

CLINT   Otherwise she wouldn't have spent/all that time
             there.

BETTE   Hitler was a man. Does that mean all men are
             like him?

CLINT   But he was a German.

BETTE   What do you want to do now?

             (CLINT *looks* BETTE *up and down . . . he winks,
             then unbuttons his shirt as if hot.*)

BETTE   You've got a good body. But you've got a sick
             mind. (*Pause.*) But you've got a good body.

             (CLINT *continues to unbutton his shirt.*)

BETTE   You've got a nice face.

             (CLINT *removes his shirt.* BETTE *touches his
             body.*)

BETTE   You've got a great body.

             (BETTE'S *hand goes down to his trousers and
             rests on his zip.*)

BETTE   Ah well, you can't have everything.

             (BETTE *and* CLINT *exit together.*)

                          Interval

Scene Eleven

*The beach. Morning. During the interval litter has
accumulated on the beach.* MARILYN'S *voice can be heard
offstage.* MARILYN *enters from the right with a ball found on
the plane.*

MARILYN   I won't travel with that airline again. I checked
            in at Terminal Three. For a start I don't think
            anything in an airport should be called terminal -
            doesn't put you in the right frame of mind. We
            took off and at first everything was fine. Then
            we met the storm. Suddenly my eyes were in the
            back of my head. The plane was in a dive.
            Straight down like that. Those who believed in
            God started to pray. Those who didn't believe in
            God, they started to pray. There are no atheists
            at 30,000 feet. Are you coming or what?

            (MERYL *is still offstage.*)

MERYL   Yes!

MARILYN   Come on then!

MERYL   I can't!

MARILYN   You're not trying.

MERYL   I am.

MARILYN   It's easy when you get the hang of it.

MERYL   It's impossible.

MARILYN   Come on.

            (MERYL *enters from the right wearing high-
            heeled shoes in which she makes tottering
            progress.*)

MERYL   Which people are made to wear these?
            Criminals?

MARILYN   Everyone wears them.

MERYL   Do men wear them?

MARILYN   No.

MERYL   So who wears them?

MARILYN   Women.

MERYL   Why?

MARILYN   Come on, you've got to do another half mile.

MERYL   Were they invented by a woman?

MARILYN   I don't know.

MERYL   Do women in every country wear them?

MARILYN   No, only the advanced cultures.

MERYL   What about the pain in the back of my legs, my
          knees, my back and my ankles?

MARILYN   You won't notice it after a bit.

MERYL   I can't walk properly.

MARILYN   You're doing alright.

MERYL   M'feet.

MARILYN   I know women who wear these while carrying
          four bags of shopping and running for a bus.

          (MERYL *exchanges the shoes for the ball. They
          toss the ball back and forth.* MARILYN
          participates in a bored way. MERYL *has the ball.*
          MARILYN *exits and* CLINT *enters.*)

                              *

          (MERYL *and* CLINT *throw the ball back and forth.*
          CLINT *moves athletically. He is showing off. On
          one occasion he throws the ball more firmly*

towards her. MERYL *catches it but* CLINT *is apologetic.*)

CLINT   Sorry. Bit too hard. Forgot.

(MERYL *throws the ball back.* CLINT *tosses it back very gently. They continue to toss it gently back and forth.* MERYL *has the ball.* CLINT *exits and* BETTE *enters.*)

                                    *

(MERYL *throws the ball to* BETTE, *who keeps hold of it.*)

BETTE   The way you walk is important. I know a woman, if there's a man walking towards her she looks down like this and doesn't look up till he's gone past. Don't walk like this. (*Demonstrates a timid walk.*) Walk like this. (*Demonstrates a confident walk, staring contemptuously at a passerby.*) Show me how you walk.

(MERYL *walks nervously.*)

BETTE   Lift your chin up.

(MERYL *walks nervously with her chin lifted up.*)

BETTE   (*tucks her arms into her side*) You're like this. You're as entitled to the pavement as anyone else. Use up more space with your arms.

(MERYL *walks nervously with her chin lifted and her arms using up some space.*)

BETTE   Tiny steps. You'll never get anywhere like that. Lengthen your stride. And take your time.

(*Chin raised, arms as if she's carrying suitcases, her stride long and leisurely,* MERYL'S *walk is a parody of male machismo and arrogance.*)

BETTE   We'll have to work on that.

MERYL   Pass the ball?

BETTE   (*mocking imitation*) Pass the ball? (*Strongly.*)
             Pass the ball!

MERYL   Pass the ball?

BETTE   Pass the ball!

MERYL   Pass the ball!

BETTE   Pass the ball!!

MERYL   Pass the ball!!

BETTE   Pass the ball!!!

MERYL   Pass the ball!!!

BETTE   Pass the ball!!!!!!

MERYL   Pass the ball!!!!!!

             (*Pause.*)

BETTE   Better.

             (BETTE *passes the ball. They throw it back and
             forth.* BETTE *holds on to it again.*)

BETTE   Who taught you to throw like that? Throw it like
             this.

             (BETTE *throws the ball back firmly.* MERYL
             *returns it firmly. They throw it firmly back and
             forth.* MERYL *has the ball.* BETTE *exits and* HENRY
             enters.)

                                   *

             (MERYL *throws the ball.* HENRY *keeps hold of it.*)

HENRY   Who's been talking to you about God? Is it that
             Marilyn?

MERYL   Yeah.

HENRY   I'm going to tell you something you must never
            forget. Beware of Christians. Especially the ones
            that talk about having a personal relationship
            with Jesus.

MERYL   Yeah?

HENRY   Christians are people who claim they're humble
            and then say that God is their personal adviser. If
            you want to learn about religion I can
            recommend something. It's called *Monty
            Python's Life Of Brian*.

MERYL   Henry.

HENRY   What?

MERYL   Pass the ball!!!

            (HENRY *passes the ball.* MERYL *has the ball.*
            HENRY *exits and* MARILYN *enters.*)

                              *

            (MERYL *throws the ball.* MARILYN *makes a feeble
            attempt to catch it.*)

MARILYN   Sorry, can't catch.

            (MARILYN'S *throw fails to reach* MERYL.)

            Sorry, can't throw.

            (MERYL *retrieves the ball.* MARILYN *exits and*
            CLINT *enters.*)

                              *

            (MERYL *and* CLINT *pass the ball back and forth
            for a while.* CLINT *is looking at* MERYL.)

MERYL   What?

CLINT   I know a better game than this one.

MERYL   Yeah?

CLINT   Oh aye. Want me to teach it to you?

MERYL   Yeah.

CLINT   We can't play it here. We have to go somewhere else. Leave the ball.

MERYL   Oh.

              (*Leaving the ball,* CLINT *and* MERYL *exit together.*)

                        *

              (BETTE *enters.* MERYL *enters. They throw the ball.*)

MERYL   I thought you said it's rude to stick your tongue out at people.

BETTE   It is.

MERYL   Clint stuck his tongue out at me.

BETTE   When did he do that?

MERYL   When he was kissing me.

BETTE   Has he been upsetting you?

MERYL   No.

BETTE   Did he force himself on you? Did he make you do things you didn't want to?

MERYL   Well, no.

BETTE   Why do you say it like that?

MERYL   He was more reluctant than I was.

BETTE   Are you sure about that?

MERYL   He wasn't the first time we did it or the second time, but he was the third time we did it. When I asked him to do it again, he told me to give him a minute or two to get his breath back. I gave him two minutes and he still wasn't ready, and he told me what a figure of speech is.

BETTE   Did he say anything to you?

MERYL   Like what?

BETTE   Did he say, you're better than so-and-so, you are?

MERYL   No.

BETTE   Did he mention anyone else?

MERYL   No.

BETTE   Did he mention me?

MERYL   No.

BETTE   What else did he do?

MERYL   He screwed his face up.

BETTE   Did you screw your face up?

MERYL   Yeah.

BETTE   What else happened?

MERYL   Er . . .

BETTE   Did he go like this?

(BETTE *touches* MERYL'S *breasts tenderly.*)

MERYL   No, it was more like this.

(MERYL *rubs* BETTE'S *breasts roughly.*)

BETTE   Bet you didn't enjoy that very much.

MERYL   No, didn't get much out of that.

BETTE   What else did he do?

MERYL   Held my hand.

BETTE   You mean like this?

MERYL   Yeah.

BETTE   What else did he do?

MERYL   Kissed me.

BETTE   You mean like this.

MERYL   No, not like that.

BETTE   Shall we go for a walk?

MERYL   If you want to.

BETTE   Do you want to?

MERYL   Yeah.

BETTE   What you've experienced is the birds and the bees. I'm going to tell you about the birds and the birds.

MERYL   I won't bring the ball.

BETTE   No, leave it behind.

(*Leaving the ball,* BETTE *and* MERYL *exit right.* HENRY *enters from the left and waits with the ball.*)

*

HENRY   Come on. Come on. Hurry up.

(MERYL *enters from the right.*)

MERYL   Sorry.

HENRY   You can't just go off like that.

MERYL   It was Clint.

HENRY   I know who it was.

MERYL   He's going swimming.

HENRY   So?

MERYL   Sorry.

HENRY   What was I saying?

MERYL   Christians.

HENRY   What you have to remember is that the Bible has
            gone beyond its sell-by date. There should be a
            label on the cover saying, "Best before the
            sixteenth century."

MERYL   Look, he's going into the water.

HENRY   Don't you want to know about this?

MERYL   He teaches me things.

HENRY   I can imagine what he teaches you.

MERYL   He's my friend.

HENRY   Friendship is a meeting of minds, not of genitals.

MERYL   Have you got any friends, Henry?

HENRY   I've had sex you know! I lived with a woman
            once. It was good. But then it wasn't. We were
            still having orgasms at the same time, but while I
            was having mine in Wigan she was having hers
            in St Helens. There's an old saying, "is that a
            gun in your pocket or are you just pleased to see
            me?" When you first meet them, you are pleased
            to see them. When you've lived with them for
            two years, it is a gun. Marriage is a permanent
            contract based on temporary feelings — casual
            sex is a temporary contract based on permanent
            feelings. In a 1952 film called *Moulin Rouge*,
            marriage is compared to a dull meal with the
            dessert at the beginning.

MERYL   He said he'll teach me how to swim. He's good,
            isn't he? Can you swim like that?

HENRY   I can swim.

MERYL   Like that?

         (*Their heads turn as* CLINT *speeds across the sea
         in front of them.*)

HENRY   I can swim.

MERYL   He's very fast.

HENRY   Yes. Every quality of a dolphin except
         intelligence.

MERYL   Why does his body look like that and yours
         doesn't?

HENRY   He looks as if he's done body-building.

MERYL   He's built it very well. Don't you wish he'd built
         yours?

HENRY   That's the problem with body-building. It has to
         be DIY. You can't get someone in to do it for
         you.

MERYL   What does it do?

HENRY   It raises the veins in the muscles of his arms. It
         creates the shapeliness of his legs. It preserves
         the slimness of his hips. It keeps his bottom
         small and tight so that each buttock fits snugly
         into the palm of a hand.

MERYL   Henry.

HENRY   What?

MERYL   I know about the birds and the birds. What about
         the bees and the bees?

HENRY   What are you talking about?

MERYL   Can men like men?

HENRY   Yes.

MERYL   Henry.

HENRY   What?

MERYL   What do you like?

HENRY   I like football. I would have been a footballer but I was no good.

MERYL   What's that got to do with it?

HENRY   Well, I don't call myself a footballer. Because I don't play. So how can I call myself a heterosexual? Or whatever? I might as well call myself an astronaut because that's also something I'd like to do if I got the chance.

             (*A pause as they watch* CLINT *swimming past.*)

MERYL   Are you bored?

HENRY   I think we're all in the company of people whom, in other circumstances, we'd arrange our lives to avoid.

MERYL   I know something we can do. Do you mind?

             (MERYL *begins to undo the fly on* HENRY'S *trousers.*)

HENRY   I have the gravest doubts upon the subject but I intend to crush them. That's a line from the 1953 version of *The Importance of Being Earnest.* Margaret Rutherford. Edith Evans. Michael Redgrave. Joan Greenwood.

             (MERYL *is still fiddling with* HENRY'S *fly.*)

HENRY   Listen.

MERYL   What?

HENRY   There's something you ought to know.

MERYL   What?

HENRY   I'm easily excited.

MERYL   What do you mean, easily?

HENRY   No, listen.

MERYL   What?

HENRY   Have you heard of premature ejaculation?

MERYL   No, I haven't.

HENRY   Listen.

MERYL   What?

HENRY   I've come.

MERYL   Already?

HENRY   I said it was premature. I'm sorry.

MERYL   This didn't happen when I did it with Clint.
         When I did it with him/

HENRY   I don't want to hear about him.

MERYL   Do you want to throw the ball?

HENRY   Yes, I don't mind.

         (HENRY *and* MERYL *pass the ball back and forth.*)

MERYL   I wish I could swim.

HENRY   It's supposed to be good for you.

MERYL   He's going to teach me.

HENRY   Well, you be careful.

MERYL   Is it dangerous?

HENRY   Not really. As long as you conquer your fear and
         don't go out of your depth.

MERYL   Can you swim as well as he can?

HENRY   No, but I can read and write.

MERYL   Can't he read and write?

HENRY   No, he can't.

Scene Twelve

MERYL *has the ball. She keeps hold of it. It is afternoon on the beach.* MERYL *and* HENRY *occupy themselves unobtrusively.* MARILYN *and* CLINT *enter from the left and stroll across stage.*

MARILYN   Shoes, skirts, scarves, jeans, jacket — khaki long-sleeved crew-necked sweater, camel short-sleeved top, wild rose polo neck, cashmere blazer. Everything's in my suitcase.

CLINT   But your suitcase is where my suitcase is.

MARILYN   That's right. Among the cargo.

CLINT   And we can't open the hatch. There's a massive rock in the way.

MARILYN   Yes, but I've had an idea.

CLINT   What idea?

MARILYN   Move the rock.

CLINT   I can't move the rock.

MARILYN   With your muscles? Popeye would have to eat a lot of spinach to look like you.

CLINT   It's a big rock.

MARILYN   Everything's in my suitcase. My fishnet tights. My black satin. My lace underwear. Everything.

CLINT   I'll see what I can do.

MARILYN   My silky trousers, my jogging trousers, my T-shirts, my cycling shorts, my denim waistcoat,

my tight Levis, my cotton sweater with a starfish
pattern . . .

(MARILYN'S *list continues as she and* CLINT *exit*
right and continues as she re-enters immediately
from the right with BETTE.)

MARILYN   . . . My mushroom-coloured dress, my dusky
pink cardigan, my salmon-pink hat, my tobacco-
coloured single-breasted jacket, my black and
white checked top with matching skirt, and all
my tights.

BETTE   What do you expect him to do?

MARILYN   I've got this dress, wait till you see it.

BETTE   There's no way he can budge that rock.

MARILYN   Aw, don't say that.

BETTE   Have you seen the size of it?

MARILYN   Give him a chance.

BETTE   He's been pushing it for an hour.

(CLINT *enters from the right.*)

MARILYN   Well?

BETTE   Have you done it then?

MARILYN   Where's my suitcase?

BETTE   Well?

CLINT   I need a volunteer.

BETTE   Me?

CLINT   Man's job.

(HENRY *sighs.*)

Henry.

MARILYN   Henry, you're wanted.

HENRY   Clint, you're/much better with inanimate objects than I am. My methods are rational argument and persuasion. I can't negotiate with a rock.

ALL   Henry/Henry/Henry/Come on, Henry/Henry/ Henry . . .

(*Etc* — HENRY *submits to the pressure.*)

HENRY   Oh dear.

CLINT   Good man.

HENRY   It won't do any good.

CLINT   Don't talk like that. Get in there. Grit your teeth. Put your shoulder in. Head down. Go for it. Get stuck in. Give it a bit of welly. Don't take no for an answer. Show it who's boss.

HENRY   I'm not very good at that sort of thing.

(CLINT *and* HENRY *exit right.*)

MARILYN   I've got these leggings that are a combination of cotton and lycra.

(HENRY *enters from the right.*)

MARILYN   Well?

HENRY   Can't do it.

MARILYN   Are you sure?

HENRY   Can't do it.

MARILYN   Is there no chance?

HENRY   No chance.

BETTE   What happened?

HENRY   I told him after one push it wouldn't move. But the wanker wouldn't listen to me. Half an hour we were pushing this enormous rock. A waste of fucking time. "Push it. Push it." Fuck off. Fucking dickhead. Fuck him.

(CLINT *enters from the right, devastated by his failure.*)

BETTE Well?

CLINT What?

BETTE Any luck?

CLINT Not possible. Did what I could.

MARILYN Oh dear.

BETTE Oh dear. How far did you manage to move the rock?

CLINT Didn't.

BETTE Sorry?

CLINT We didn't move the rock.

BETTE Not even an inch?

CLINT No.

BETTE Sorry?

CLINT No.

BETTE So it was a complete failure?

CLINT Yes.

BETTE Sorry?

CLINT Yes.

BETTE They can't do it.

MARILYN I heard.

BETTE It was a complete failure, apparently.

MARILYN My skirts. My jeans.

BETTE　　　Tell you what.

MARILYN　　What?

BETTE　　　We'll do it.

MARILYN　　What can we do?

BETTE　　　Come on.

(BETTE *and* MARILYN *exit right. It becomes darker. It is night.*)

HENRY　　　Heh.

CLINT　　　What?

HENRY　　　Listen. This might be none of my business. You're upset, aren't you?

CLINT　　　That's right, it is none of your business.

HENRY　　　When it rained last night I didn't get wet. Those shelters you built, they're very good. I admire people who can make things with their hands. I admire what they make, anyway. What I'm saying is, I didn't get wet when it rained last night.

(MARILYN *enters holding a favourite dress.* BETTE *enters and distributes goodies to the others . . . clothes to* HENRY *and* CLINT *and a walkman to* MERYL *. . . meanwhile* MARILYN *and* BETTE *celebrate their triumph loudly . . . each word is exclaimed at length.*)

MARILYN　　Done it!

BETTE　　　Done it!

MARILYN　　You should see it!

BETTE　　　Told you!

MARILYN　　Look what I've got!

BETTE   There's everything we need!

MARILYN   Isn't it gorgeous!

BETTE   Told you!

MARILYN   And there's more!

BETTE   Told you!

> (*The distribution happens very quickly . . .*
> MARILYN *and* BETTE *exit.* HENRY *examines the*
> *shirt he has been given . . .* CLINT *is too*
> *humiliated to be bothered with his . . .* MERYL *is*
> *listening to the walkman. Eyes closed,* MERYL
> *starts to hum along to her walkman . . . The song*
> *is 'Summertime (And the Living is Easy)' . . . In*
> *a world of her own, she is humming without a*
> *sense that she is being listened to.* CLINT *stares*
> *at her . . . stands over her.* MERYL *opens her eyes*
> *. . . sees* CLINT *. . . stops humming.*)

CLINT   Noisy little bitch. Do you want to feel the back
            of my hand across your face? I can break your
            nose. I can make your eyes bleed. I can make
            your knees bend the other way. I can rip the hair
            out of your head. I'm bigger than you are. I'm
            stronger than you are. Shall I slap my knuckles
            against your soft face? Shall I pulp your peach
            head, shall I kick your cucumber spine, shall I
            break your brittle bones? I can fuck you. Is that
            what you want? Is that what I have to do? My
            hands would fit round your neck. I could put my
            thumbs over your eyes and squeeze. Bitch.

HENRY   Clint.

MERYL   He wouldn't hit me.

HENRY   He would.

MERYL   He's so polite normally.

HENRY   It's said that Gary Cooper always took his hat off
            when he was hitting a woman.

Scene Thirteen

The beach. Morning. The lights brighten as the day gets hotter. The characters prepare themselves and the stage for the next scene.

A party on the beach . . . everyone is dressed in smart clothes found among the cargo. In this context they look comically absurd. Empty bottles reveal that most of the duty free has been consumed. BETTE *is reading a copy of the Guardian which she has found on the plane . . .* CLINT *is still sulking, and during this scene he comes to regard everyone with a brooding hatred, exasperated by their chatter . . .* MERYL *is surrounded by the debris of indulgence . . . both drink and food . . . she has a compulsion to eat . . . food is clumped and smeared around her mouth . . . the walkman headphones are around her neck . . . she is eating a biscuit.*

CLINT   (*insistence*) Come on then, tell me.

BETTE   (*insouciance*) What?

CLINT   How you did it.

BETTE   Did what?

CLINT   The rock.

BETTE   Oh that.

CLINT   Come on.

BETTE   What you do, you use small pieces of wood.

CLINT   Oh yeah?

BETTE   You take small pieces of dry wood and you insert them into cracks in the rock. Then you pour water on to the wood. This causes the wood to become swollen and the rock splits, demonstrating the enormous power of expansion when water is added to dry wood. The Egyptians used to do it to stone when they were building pyramids.

      (*Pause.*)

MERYL   I feel sick.

MARILYN   You should swallow a spoonful of honey.

MERYL   Will it stop me being sick?

MARILYN   No, but it means it tastes better when it comes
             back up.

HENRY   Whose idea was it to have a party?

MARILYN   We might as well enjoy ourselves while we're
             here.

HENRY   Your idea?

MARILYN   Just went along with everyone else.

HENRY   There's no whisky left.

MARILYN   Drink vodka.

HENRY   There's no vodka left.

MARILYN   Drink rum.

HENRY   There's no rum left.

MARILYN   What about the Bacardi?

HENRY   No Bacardi left.

MARILYN   Are you sure about the Bacardi?

HENRY   And we're running out of food.

             (*Pause.*)

MERYL   Is it normal to feel sick?

MARILYN   Yes, it's normal.

MERYL   Do you feel sick?

MARILYN   Of course. Has anyone seen that advert for
             Bacardi? It says, "The view from the Dog &

Duck, Neasden, after a bottle of Bacardi". And
there's a picture of a tropical beach, palm trees
and that sort of thing. But it's not true. I've just
had a bottle of Bacardi and I feel like I'm in
Neasden.

(*Regardless of her sickness,* MERYL *is about to
put a final piece of biscuit in her mouth.*)

HENRY   Eating biscuits again?

(MERYL *stops chomping . . . tries to look innocent
but looks guilty.*)

HENRY   It's a biscuit, isn't it, the last of the biscuits.
There's no biscuits left now, you've eaten all the
biscuits, you've eaten everything, don't you
understand?

(MERYL *starts to chew slowly.*)

HENRY   It's a disaster, what is it?

MERYL   A disaster.

HENRY   And it's your fault. Whose fault is it?

MERYL   Mine.

HENRY   I hope you feel culpable. What do you feel?

MERYL   Culpable.

HENRY   What you going to do about it?

MERYL   Eat something.

(MERYL *puts the last bit of biscuit in her mouth
and starts to munch . . . then she places the
headphones over her ears and turns on the
walkman. Pause.* MARILYN *looks at* BETTE *reading
the Guardian.*)

MARILYN   Bette. (BETTE *ignores her.*) You're not much
company. What you reading that for?

BETTE   Go on then. Give me details and informed
             comment about current events in the Middle
             East, South America, North America, Europe and
             the Far East. Give me eyewitness accounts of all
             last night's football matches and the three plays
             you saw. What did the Prime Minister say when
             you interviewed him? Show me the photographs
             you took and then give me the weather forecast.
             Then give me the crossword you've compiled,
             and the answers to the one you gave me
             yesterday.

MARILYN   I've had that all my life. Because of my good
             looks people think . . .

             (MARILYN *expresses with a gesture what people
             think*.)

CLINT   I know what you mean.

MARILYN   As if I haven't got a brain in my head.

CLINT   I know.

MARILYN   Just because I'm beautiful doesn't mean I'm
             stupid.

CLINT   I know.

MARILYN   But that's what they assume.

CLINT   You have to take it philosophically. My
             philosophy is this: fuck 'em.

BETTE   Didn't say you were stupid.

MARILYN   But that was the, er . . . that was the . . . er . . .

BETTE   Implication.

MARILYN   I know. I'm joking. You must/think I'm really
             thick.

BETTE   I'm just reading my paper.

             (*Pause*.)

MARILYN   I like a Daily Male myself.

(*Pause.* MARILYN *smiles at her own joke which nobody else has noticed.*)

MARILYN   What you reading?

BETTE   It's a review of a biography of Sophocles.

MARILYN   You like biographies?

BETTE   A good review means you don't have to read the biography. It gives you the juicy bits.

CLINT   Has it got Garfield in that newspaper?

BETTE   No.

(*Pause.* MERYL *is in her walkman world. She hums an upbeat tune. Her voice fades away.*)

MARILYN   Henry, you know what you were saying?

HENRY   What?

MARILYN   That we're all characters in a film.

HENRY   It's true.

MARILYN   Pff. What kind of a film is this?

HENRY   I didn't say it was well written. If I look at my life I get the impression it's a bad first draft. It lacks dramatic structure. It hasn't got a sense of narrative purpose. But I can just about accept that. It's Christians who have difficulty reconciling their beliefs with reality. They look at the world and there's leukaemia and cancer and so much futile suffering, and they conclude that the world is governed by an omnipotent God who loves all of us. I once saw a woman with no left side to her face because cancer had — why does God allow that? The fact is, we're all characters in someone's film. He looks at the script and he thinks, what can I do to them now?

Nothing we can do about it. What's the
difference between God and a terrorist? You can
negotiate with a terrorist. Things become clear
when you realise that we're all characters in a
film. It isn't comforting but that's how it is.
Christians say they have the peace that passeth
all understanding. What I have is the
understanding that passeth all peace.

MERYL   Henry.

HENRY   What?

MERYL   Why do you talk so much?

HENRY   Well, what elevates us above other animals is
our ability to reason and to articulate ideas. The
irony of the human condition is that our intellect
doesn't enable us to solve our predicament, only
to be aware of it and to describe it at length.

(CLINT *sighs loudly to indicate his irritation.*)

But you have to know when to shut up.

(*Pause.*)

You don't want to end up like Christians.

(*Pause.*)

Christians and politicians — people who think
you're entitled not to your own opinion but to
theirs.

(*Pause.*)

They go on and on.

(MERYL *begins to hum again. Her humming and
percussion noises and finger-clicking provide a
musical accompaniment for the scene.* CLINT *does
press-ups on the floor. He stops.*)

People like Clint are useful.

BETTE   If something needs to be constructed.

HENRY   Or carried.

BETTE   Or killed. People like him come in handy.

HENRY   But what about the rest of the time?

BETTE   How do we keep them out of trouble?

HENRY   It's the education system.

BETTE   We don't have an education system, we have schooling.

HENRY   That's right.

BETTE   We rely on schools to produce an undereducated underclass of people . . .

HENRY   . . . to do the jobs the rest of us won't do.

(CLINT *parades his fist and speaks ominously.*)

CLINT   Shut your mouth, shut your mouth, shut your mouth, shut your fucking mouth, shut your fucking mouth or I'll fucking . . .

(*Pause.*)

HENRY   Why are you so aggressive?

CLINT   I can't help my nature.

HENRY   Nature is what we're put on this earth to rise above. As Katharine Hepburn tells Humphrey Bogart in *The African Queen.*

CLINT   I wake up and I hear your voice. I go to sleep and hear your voice. I'm fucking sick of your voice.

(CLINT *has the manner of a madman as he shows his fist threateningly.*)

HENRY   Never at a loss for fists.

(*Pause.* MARILYN *tuts at* CLINT.)

MARILYN   Ttt.

CLINT   Slut.

MARILYN   What are you?

CLINT   I'm a Ladies' Man.

BETTE   Some of us —

CLINT   And you can shut up an' all.

BETTE   Can I say something?

CLINT   No.

BETTE   One sentence.

CLINT   You, one sentence?

BETTE   Some of us dont want Mr Right; we want Mr
            Right Now; because when it's the first time with
            someone it's exciting; but when it's the tenth
            time, it's not quite as exciting; and when it's the
            hundredth time . . . well, I wouldn't know.

CLINT   That's ten sentences.

BETTE   I was using semi-colons.

            (*The conversation disintegrates into an exchange
            of disdainful tutting, contemptuous noises and
            abuse.*)

ALL   Ttt/Ttt/Ttt/Ttt/Ttt/Ttt/Yaaarr/Yaaarr/Yaaaaarrr/
            Yaaaarr/Fuck off/You fuck off/Fuck you/Fuck
            off/Fuck you, etc.

            (*Pause.* MERYL *continues to hum . . . more
            tunefully now.*)

HENRY   We're not getting on very well.

BETTE   No.

MARILYN   Come on, it's a party.

HENRY   In one of his films Woody Allen compares life to a restaurant. The food in this restaurant is awful, says one customer. Yes, says the other customer, and such small portions. Implying that strife is a paradox because there's a lot to recommend it. As Orson Welles says in the 1949 version of *The Third Man*, "In Italy for thirty years under the Borgias they had warfare, terror, murder, bloodshed — they produced Michelangelo, Leonardo da Vinci and the Renaissance. In Switzerland they had brotherly love, five hundred years of democracy and peace and what did they produce? The cuckoo clock."

BETTE   It's not good to have it too easy.

HENRY   That's right.

BETTE   If suffering didn't exist it would have to be invented.

MARILYN   It has been. It's called aerobics.

BETTE   The purpose of life is Sensation, wrote Byron. To feel that we exist, even in pain.

HENRY   Have you read Byron?

BETTE   I've read a review of his biography.

(*In* CLINT'S *head an idea has slowly formed.*)

CLINT   What I'm going to do is divide up the beach. We're all going to have our own space and we're all going to keep to our own space. Then what I'm going to do is chop down trees. Then what I'm going to do is build walls around my space.

MARILYN   Go on then.

BETTE   Suits me.

MARILYN   Off you go.

BETTE   If you can't love, then avoid thy neighbour.

            (CLINT *exits right.*)

            What's the best thing that human beings have
            invented?

MARILYN   The wheel.

BETTE   No, the wall.

            (MERYL's *humming merges with the next scene . . .
            she has withdrawn into a private world of music
            and for the rest of the play her humming provides
            background harmony and a link between scenes.*)

Scene Fourteen

HENRY, BETTE, MARILYN *and* MERYL *on the beach after the
party.* HENRY *is lying back and seems to be asleep.* MERYL's
humming fades.

HENRY   Did you see the way he looked at me?

MARILYN   I know.

HENRY   I thought he was going to kill me.

BETTE   We could have him. If we all jumped him at
            once.

HENRY   Seventy seven is a good page. Some characters
            don't last that long. But I want to see a hundred
            and beyond.

MARILYN   He's lucky you didn't lose your temper.

HENRY   He is.

MARILYN   I thought you might stand up and smack him one.

HENRY   I nearly did. But I told myself that isn't what
            Henry Fonda would do.

BETTE   Henry, you are an example to us all.

HENRY	Thank you.
BETTE	I mean that.
HENRY	Thank you.
BETTE	You were marvellous.
MARILYN	Defiant.
BETTE	But dignified.
MARILYN	Dignified.
BETTE	But defiant.
MARILYN	Marvellous.
HENRY	Well he'd better not try it again or I might have to teach him a lesson.
MARILYN	Watch out, he's coming back.
HENRY	Eh?
BETTE	If he starts anything, we'll all go for him.

(CLINT *enters*.)

CLINT	Henry.
HENRY	What?
CLINT	I apologise for what I said and the way I behaved.
HENRY	Go on.
CLINT	Forgive me.
HENRY	On your knees. (CLINT *falls to his knees*.) Stand up. (CLINT *stands up*.) On your knees. (CLINT *falls to his knees*.) Stand up. (CLINT *stands up*.) I forgive you.
CLINT	Three cheers for Henry! Hip hip!
ALL	Hurrah!

CLINT   Hip hip!

ALL   Hurrah!

CLINT   Hip hip!

ALL   Hurrah!

CLINT   For he's a jolly good fellow . . .

ALL   For he's a jolly good fellow,
          For he's a jolly good fellow,
          And so say all of us!
          And so say all of us,
          And so say all of us,
          For he's a jolly good fellow,
          For he's a jolly good fellow . . .

          (HENRY *waves away the song. Everyone applauds*
          HENRY.)

HENRY   Well it's very nice of you.

BETTE   We just want you to know how much we admire
          you.

MARILYN   And respect you, Henry.

CLINT   And love you, Henry.

HENRY   Kind of you to say so.

BETTE   We hold you in the highest esteem.

CLINT   You're a great guy.

HENRY   I thought you all thought I talked too much.

ALL   No!/No!/No!/No way!/What makes you think
          that?/What gave you that idea?/No way!/Never!/
          Certainly not!/No!/No!

CLINT   For he's a jolly good fellow . . .

ALL   For he's a jolly good fellow,
          For he's a jolly good fellow,

And so say all of us!
And so say all of us . . .

(*They applaud for a moment.*)

HENRY   My life hasn't always been like this. I'm the first
           to admit, I'm not much to look at.

ALL   Oh come on!/That's not true!/How can you say
           that?/He's so modest!/Come off it!/You're not
           serious?/No!/No way!/I wouldn't say that!/No!

MARILYN   Henry, you must be aware of the feelings I have
           for you?

HENRY   What feelings?

MARILYN   You're a very attractive man.

BETTE   A fine figure of a man.

HENRY   How long have you felt like this?

MARILYN   Soon as I met you.

BETTE   First time I saw you.

MARILYN   It was the eyes.

BETTE   The mouth.

MARILYN   The bum.

BETTE   The way he walks.

MARILYN   The broad chest.

BETTE   The strong hands.

MARILYN   The sensitive neck.

BETTE   What a hunk.

MARILYN   What a guy.

BETTE   He's all man.

MARILYN   You make my knees buckle.

BETTE   My thighs ache.

MARILYN   My knickers wet.

BETTE   You can't have failed to notice.

MARILYN   You must have known.

HENRY   I had no idea. I really didn't.

BETTE   And now . . .

MARILYN   And now . . .

BETTE   As a special treat . . .

MARILYN   As a special treat . . .

            (BETTE *and* MARILYN *start to hum the stripper
            song and click their fingers.* CLINT *starts to strip
            . . . his shirt is off . . . he starts to remove his
            trousers.*)

MARILYN   Henry. Henry. Wake up, Henry. Henry. Wake up.

HENRY   Five minutes. Five more minutes.

MARILYN   Henry. Wake up.

HENRY   Two more minutes.

MARILYN   Henry.

HENRY   One more minute.

            (CLINT *withdraws and exits. The stripper song
            fades away.* HENRY *falls back so that he is lying
            down in a position similar to the opening of the
            scene.* HENRY *wakes up.* MERYL *starts to hum
            again . . . quietly.*)

MARILYN   Henry. Henry. Henry.

HENRY   It was another dream.

MARILYN   Sorry.

HENRY   And it was just getting interesting.

MARILYN   Yeah?

HENRY   It was . . . stupid really. It started off with Clint
            going mad and saying he was going to divide up
            the beach.

BETTE   No, that was true.

MARILYN   He's over there now.

BETTE   We told him we want our share of the food.

MARILYN   But he won't let us.

BETTE   He won't let us.

MARILYN   We told him we want our share of the food.

            (*They look towards* CLINT *offstage in the
            distance.*)

Scene Fifteen

HENRY, BETTE, MARILYN *and* MERYL *on the beach.* MERYL *stops
accompanying her song.*

MARILYN   I'll talk to him.

HENRY   No. I'll talk to him.

MARILYN   He won't listen to you.

HENRY   You think he'll listen to you?

            (MARILYN *stands seductively showing off her
            legs, and* HENRY *has to concede that* CLINT *would
            pay attention.*)

            You remind me of Mae West. Who said it's
            better to be looked over than overlooked. But
            physical beauty is a passing thing, a transitory
            possession. So you also remind me of Norma
            Desmond. You know, from *Sunset Boulevard*.
            They used to refer to her as "The Beautiful

Norma Desmond." Then they referred to her as "Norma Desmond". Then they didn't refer to her at all.

MARILYN   I'll talk to him.

BETTE   (*threateningly*) I'll 'talk' to him.

MARILYN   No!

BETTE   Negotiation has it's place. But so does a punch in the face.

(BETTE *starts to walk across the beach towards* CLINT.)

MARILYN   Henry, tell her.

HENRY   Humans make illogical decisions. As Spock said.

(CLINT *enters and confronts* BETTE.)

CLINT   NO!

BETTE   What?

CLINT   SEE THIS LINE HERE?

BETTE   No.

CLINT   This line *here*.

BETTE   Nothing there.

CLINT   There's a line going all the way along here, around there and round the other side. /You don't cross that line. You stay on that side of the line. I don't want to see you on my side of the line.

BETTE   I don't see any line. There is no line. Don't tell me where I can walk.

(*Pause.*)

BETTE   I'll go where I like.

CLINT   You won't.

BETTE	I will.
CLINT	You won't cross that line.
BETTE	(*imitating* CLINT) "You won't cross that line . . ."
CLINT	Aye. (*He nods.*)
BETTE	Aye. (*She nods.*)
CLINT	Aye. (*He nods.*)
BETTE	Aye. (*She nods.*)
CLINT	Yaaar. (*He nods.*)
BETTE	Yaaar. (*She nods.*)
CLINT	Yaaar. (*He nods.*)
BETTE	Yaaar. (*She nods.*)

(*He nods. She nods.*
He nods. She nods.
He nods. She nods.
He nods. She nods.
He nods. She nods.
He nods. She nods.
They continue to nod alternately.)

CLINT	I can go on forever.

(BETTE *says nothing as they continue to nod alternately.*)

I'm not giving up.

(BETTE *says nothing as they continue to nod alternately.*)

Count of three. One. Two. Three.

(*On the third count they nod at the same time to end the contest without dishonour. They stare at each other.*)

BETTE	Where's the line?

CLINT   About an inch in front of your feet.

BETTE   What, there?

CLINT   That's right.

           (BETTE *takes one step forward.*)

BETTE   Where's the line?

CLINT   About an inch in front of your feet.

BETTE   You just said it was there.

CLINT   I'm giving you a chance.

BETTE   So where is it now?

CLINT   Anyone crosses the line, I'll shoot them.

BETTE   Where's the line?

CLINT   About an inch in front of your feet.

           (BETTE *takes one step forward.* CLINT *stares for a moment. He turns and exits.*)

BETTE   See me? See what happens when you stand up to them?

           (*From offstage there is a loud gunshot.* BETTE *takes a step back.* CLINT *enters with a smoking gun.*)

CLINT   I told you to get back.

BETTE   I am back.

CLINT   Behind the line.

BETTE   I am.

CLINT   You're not.

BETTE   Where's the line?

CLINT   About an inch behind your feet.

(BETTE *takes another step back.* MERYL *is listening to a Beatles song . . . "Can't Buy Me Love" . . . which she starts to sing aloud.*)

BETTE   Okay?

CLINT   Next time.

BETTE   What, you'll aim for my head?

CLINT   I was aiming for your head. Next time I won't miss. (CLINT *waves the gun.*) I'm not used to this gun. It could go off accidentally. Better keep out of my way.

Scene Sixteen

After a verse of "Can't Buy Me Love", MERYL *has stopped the song.* HENRY, BETTE, MARILYN *and* MERYL *on the beach.*

HENRY   What we've got to remember is that things are never as bad for us as they were for Scarlet O'Hara in *Gone With the Wind*. Her mother had typhoid, her father was insane. A man tried to kill her so she had to shoot him in the face. She was attacked by a mob. The man she loved was married to someone called Melanie. Her father was killed when he fell off a horse. Her daughter Bonnie was killed when she fell off a horse. And when Scarlet said to Clark Gable, "What will become of me?" Clark Gable turned to her and said, "Frankly, my dear, I don't give a damn." But Scarlet O'Hara was a positive thinker. "Tomorrow," she said , "is another day."

            (*Pause.*)

MARILYN   When he calms down I'm going to have a word. I'm hungry.

BETTE   After all the terrible things he said about you?

MARILYN   I don't remember that.

BETTE   He called you a slut.

MARILYN   I don't remember.

HENRY   Someone asked Ingrid Bergman for her definition
             of happiness. She said, "Good health and a bad
             memory."

MARILYN   He's got a fire going.

BETTE   Has he?

MARILYN   He's cooking.

BETTE   Is he?

             (MARILYN *sniffs the air deeply. The others cannot
             resist doing the same several times. Pause.*)

MARILYN   What's this? Two large onions, three large red
             peppers, fried gently for five minutes in three
             tablespoons of olive oil —

BETTE   Will you shut up, you?

MARILYN   It was going to be ratatouille.

BETTE   There's four of us and one of him. If we all go
             for him at once. Two of us grab his arms, one of
             us gets his legs so he can't kick, and then I can
             nip in with a small rock and smash his fucking
             head in.

MARILYN   Won't work.

BETTE   Make spears out of branches.

MARILYN   He's got the gun.

BETTE   But we all go for him at once. From all sides.

MARILYN   And he shoots us.

BETTE   We'll have to be quick.

MARILYN   I'm not doing it.

(*Pause.*)

MARILYN   Leave him to me.

BETTE   He hates you.

HENRY   Some of the best movies were made by people
            who hated each other's guts. Line from a 1952
            film called *The Bad and the Beautiful*.

MARILYN   I'm waiting till he's eaten. He'll be in a better
            mood.

HENRY   You don't have to do anything. I'm going to talk
            to him.

MARILYN   You?

HENRY   It's what Henry Fonda would do.

MARILYN   He doesn't respond to the Henry Fonda type of
            person. He responds to the Jane Fonda type of
            person.

HENRY   No, you're wrong. This is my big scene . . . give
            me the gun, Clint. Clint, give me the gun . . .

MARILYN   Henry.

HENRY   The strange thing is, my legs have gone. I'll look
            him in the eye and I'll say, "Clint, hand over that
            gun" . . . as soon as I've got the use of my legs
            again. They've got that spongy rubbery feeling. I
            don't remember Henry Fonda mentioning that in
            Twelve Angry Men. He does spend a lot of the
            time sitting down. Maybe that's why, because he
            had the spongy rubbery feeling in his legs. I'm
            ready though. To do what I have to do. Just
            waiting for my legs . . . Give me the gun, Clint.
            Clint, give me the gun . . .

            (MARILYN *and* BETTE *start to chant* HENRY'S
            name.)

MARILYN } Henry, Henry, Henry, Henry, Henry, Henry,
BETTE   } Henry . . .

HENRY   I'm ready for him. "Clint, give me the gun. The gun, Clint, give it to me. Give me the gun. Give me the gun, Clint. Clint, give me the gun . . .

         (*The chanting continues as* HENRY *moves across the beach and advances towards* CLINT.)

         Clint, give me the gun! Put the gun down! Give me the gun, Clint!

ALL   Henry, Henry, Henry, Henry . . .

         (HENRY *exits. There is a loud shot offstage.*)

         HENRY!

         (MERYL *hums another bit of the tune of "Can't Buy Me Love" . . . more slowly.*)

Scene Seventeen

The beach. MERYL *stops humming the song.* BETTE, MARILYN *and* MERYL *are sniffing the air deeply for the fumes from* CLINT'S *cooking.*

BETTE   Meat.

MARILYN   Can't be meat. There was no meat. We ran out of meat. You're hallucinating. (*She sniffs deeply. It is meat.*) Where's he got meat from?

         (*Pause.*)

MARILYN   I'm off. How do I look? Good enough to eat?

BETTE   Like a tart. Don't go.

MARILYN   I'm starving.

BETTE   What are you going to do?

MARILYN   Talk to him.

BETTE   And?

MARILYN   Show him a bit of leg. Stand close so he can
            smell me. Laugh at his jokes.

            (MARILYN *laughs and stops as abruptly as she
            began.*)

BETTE   Oh he'll love that.

MARILYN   It seems to work.

            (*Pause.*)

BETTE   Smile at him and he'll give you stale bread.
            Laugh at his jokes and he'll give you butter. But
            what will you have to do for the cheese?

MARILYN   We tried your way. It didn't work.

BETTE   It was a moral victory.

MARILYN   What use is that? Only losers claim moral
            victories. It's nothing to be proud of. Julius
            Caesar didn't say, "I came, I saw, I had a moral
            victory". You can always recognise a moral
            victor. It's the one on the floor bleeding. Better
            to be an immoral victor.

BETTE   Submit to him? I'd rather . . .

MARILYN   What, die?

BETTE   No, kill him.

MARILYN   An eye for an eye makes the whole world blind.

BETTE   I was thinking more of two eyes for an eye.

            (MARILYN *exits in the direction of* CLINT. *As she
            goes she calls his name.*)

MARILYN   Clint . . . Clint . . .

The End